12 EASY MASTER SOLO GUITAR

Complete Classical Guitar Arrangements in Standard Notation & Tab

BY STEVE PEPLIN

ISBN 9798738786181

HOW TO GET THE AUDIO

The audio files for this book are available for free as downloads or streaming on *troynelsonmusic.com*.

We are available to help you with your audio downloads and any other questions you may have. Simply email *help@troynelsonmusic.com*.

See below for the recommended ways to listen to the audio:

Download Audio Files (Zipped)	Stream Audio Files
• Download Audio Files (Zipped)	• Recommended for CELL PHONES & TABLETS
• Recommended for COMPUTERS on WiFi	• Bookmark this page
• A ZIP file will automatically download to the default "downloads" folder on your computer	• Simply tap the PLAY button on the track you want to listen to
• Recommended: download to a desktop/laptop computer *first*, then transfer to a tablet or cell phone	• Files also available for streaming or download at *soundcloud.com/troynelsonbooks*
• Phones & tablets may need an "unzipping" app such as iZip, Unrar or Winzip	
• Download on WiFi for faster download speeds	

To download the companion audio files for this book,
visit: troynelsonmusic.com/audio-downloads/

INTRODUCTION

12 Easy Classical Masterpieces for Solo Guitar is a labor of love for me, as I've always wanted to find a book of classical works for solo guitar that treats the repertoire as "songs," or "tunes" (i.e., familiar melodies with clear chord changes), instead of inflexible arrangements whose chord changes need to be transcribed and then rendered into the antiquated figured-bass method traditionally used in classical music to indicate chord changes. Granted, I enjoy the process of all this, but the figured-bass method is outdated and slow compared to the system we enjoy today—the chord-symbol system.

In the Classical (Western art music) tradition, chord symbols are rarely employed, as these powerful harmonic tools were not invented yet, and the Classical traditions often eschew aspects of musical modernity, favoring the methods and structures employed in those days. It has always been the tradition to use figured-bass Roman numerals, a system that hasn't been common practice since 1751 and cannot fully represent the harmonies of the Classical era (1750–1820), let alone the Romantic era (1820–1900).

So now, we use chord symbols—ingenious and compact devices fully capable of representing the totality of the vertical (harmonic) and horizontal (melodic) content of a single measure. For example, a C7♭13 chord (C–E–G–B♭–A♭) tells us there is a C7 (C dominant 7 chord) harmony, with an A♭ (notated as either a ♭6th or ♭13th) in the melody.

Chord symbols are associated with popular musical traditions, especially American jazz, the mother of chord symbols. But the harmonic structures you encounter in jazz are also found in classical music, which you'll discover as you work through this book.

Chord symbols allow us to really learn these pieces as "songs," which can be more easily memorized and even improvised upon. The progenitors of these works were also great improvisors who would often get together to play variations upon each other's music, which meant they knew this repertoire—they knew the chords.

As a professional guitarist/composer/improviser, I have played numerous solo gigs for various functions—concerts, weddings, restaurant gigs, recording sessions, etc.—in many genres, but one of my favorites is the solo classical guitar gig, which is a frequent request, as this instrument offers a surprisingly vast arsenal of timbral hues, despite its rather diminutive output. I love playing classical repertoire from fakebooks (music folios with only the melody and chord symbols) because this approach brings me deeper into the harmonic construction of the music and allows room for counterpoint and improvisation.

The masters of Classical music (Bach, Beethoven, Mozart, Chopin, etc.) often changed the textures of accompaniment (block chords, arpeggiation, counterpoint, etc.) for the common repertoire of their day to adapt to the instrument being played (piano was ever the preferred instrument of the composer for its capacity for simultaneities and legato string pedaling). With that in mind, the arrangements in this folio are examples of how I might perform and improvise within these pieces (from a fakebook) during a gig specifically for solo classical guitar, offering idiomatic counterpoint, chord voicings, harmonics, and timbral considerations for this challenging and beautiful music.

The classical guitar tradition uses some terminology and techniques that need to be understood for the guitarist to get the most out of this book. So, before you dive into the arrangements, let's go over some of the most important ones here.

THE HANDS

The Fretting Hand

The fingerings of the fretting hand are numbered as follows:

Index: 1
Middle: 2
Ring: 3
Pinky: 4

Frethand fingerings are indicated in the notation, near noteheads, in special circumstances throughout this book. Too many fingerings can result in a cluttered score, however, so usage has been kept to a minimum.

The Picking Hand

The fingers of the right hand are traditionally named in Spanish, as follows:

Thumb: *pulgar* (*p*)
Index: *indice* (*i*)
Middle: *medio* (*m*)
Ring: *anular* (*a*)
Pinky (used infrequently): *chico* (*c*)

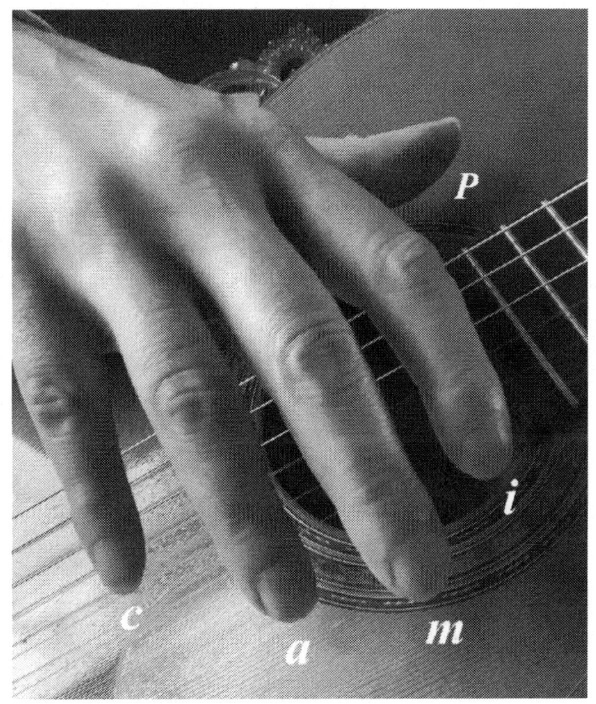

THE FINGERNAILS

Since the appearance of Andrés Segovia (1893–1987), most classical guitarists prefer to use pick-hand nails to pluck the strings. There are many schools of thought on how to position the picking hand, how to shape the nails, and even how to fabricate artificial nails. These topics are a bit too varied and multifaceted to fully cover here, and only you will be able to fully discern what is necessary for your hands and tonal preferences, but I will briefly elaborate on my preferences, for what it's worth.

Many of the great masters—Fernando Sor, Matteo Carcassi, and Francisco Tarrega, among others—did not grow out the nails of their picking hand. The reasoning for this decision is that nails tend to produce a brighter, almost metallic tone reminiscent of a harpsichord, whereas playing with the flesh of the picking hand sounds similar to a piano (darker and fuller timbres), which these masters preferred.

Personally, I prefer the tone generated by nails (which you can hear on the accompanying audio). As much as I would prefer not to have to maintain them, I find fret-hand nails useful on my electric guitars, as well, even in conjunction with a pick (plectrum).

COMMON PICKING PATTERNS

This section features a few common picking patterns that you'll encounter in this book. Spend a little time to acquaint yourself with each one.

Prelude in C Minor (Chopin) and *Carprice No. 24* (Paganini) both use the *p–i–m–i* pattern (see below).

Prelude in C Minor:

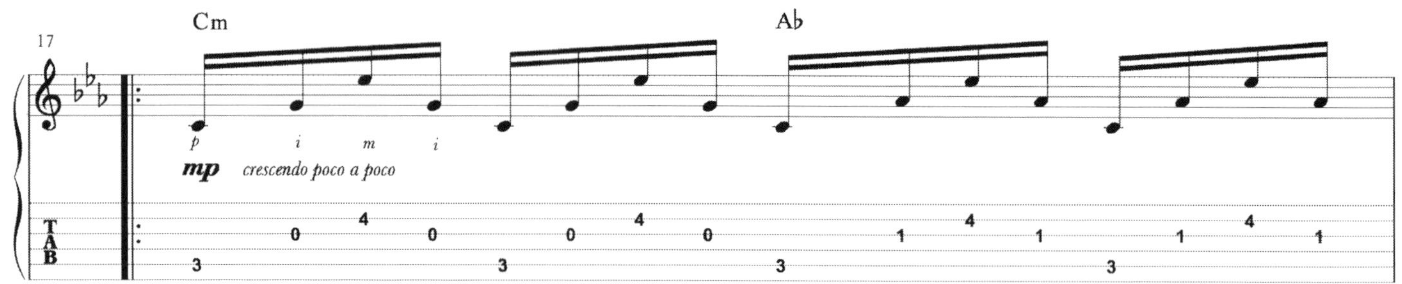

Caprice No. 24 (also *p–i–m–i*, but faster):

Caprice No. 24 uses a classic technique called *tremolo*—a rapid succession of the same note—which has been employed by all the masters. Be sure to keep your nails free of imperfections to execute this technique more easily.

Caprice No. 24 (tremolo picking):

THE REST STROKE AND THE FREE STROKE

In conventional classical guitar technique, the string can be propelled in two ways:

The Rest Stroke

After striking the string, simply rest the striking finger on the string above it (except the low-E string, where the stroke is coming from the thumb, which would put the rest stroke on the string *below* it, A).

The Free Stroke

After propelling the string, that finger (usually index or middle) does not rest on a string.

PLAYING POSTURES

Traditional Posture (Two Variations)

Foot-Stool Method

Sit towards the edge of a chair, back straight, with the left leg (right leg if playing left-handed) elevated on a guitar foot-stool. The foot stool is adjustable, so experiment with different heights of the weight-bearing leg. Meanwhile, your other leg should be positioned approximately 45 degrees from the weight-bearing leg.

Guitar-Support Method

If a foot stool is not preferred, consider a guitar support, which raises the guitar while allowing the weight-bearing leg (where the support resides) to rest on the ground.

The advantages of traditional posture are threefold:

1. The body of the guitar is unimpeded, so it resonates more.
2. The shoulders, wrists, and back are fairly straight, offering less resistance than just sitting with a guitar on your leg.
3. Since the neck is elevated, fretboard visibility is high.

Flamenco Posture (Two Variations)

Ankle-Rest Method

Sit back in your chair, resting your right leg (or the leg upon which the guitar rests) on your other leg, ankle resting just behind the opposite leg's knee.

Knee-Rest Method

Place your guitar-bearing leg over your other leg, letting the guitar-bearing leg hang from the knee joint. This technique, however, has a couple of problems: your leg will fall asleep, so you will have to reset your position frequently, and it's known to elicit back problems if overdone.

The *advantages* of the flamenco postures are twofold:

1. You don't need a footstool or guitar support.
2. It looks cool/casual, which can help the guitarist to relax.

THE ANATOMY OF THE CLASSICAL GUITAR

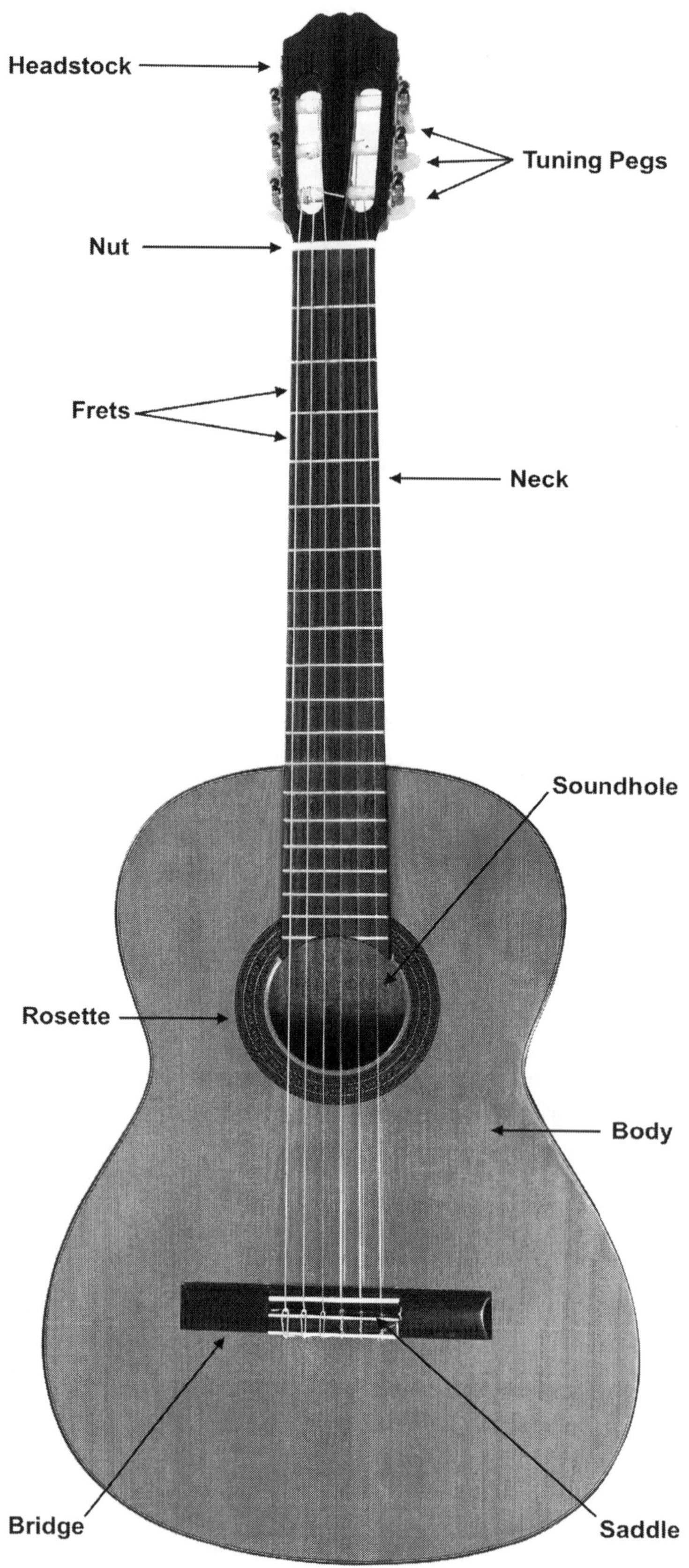

Headstock

The top portion of the guitar neck that typically houses the tuning system, the truss-rod port, and the luthier's or manufacturer's logo.

Tuning Pegs (Tuners)

Each tuning peg in the system contains a tuning head, cylinder, tuning post, bore hole, pinion gear, worm drive, bushing, button, rubber casing, and lock-in screw.

Nut

A plastic or bovine-bone ridge with carved slots. This is where the strings rest.

Neck

The shaft between the body and headstock that contains the fretboard (usually rosewood or ebony). Inside most guitar necks resides a truss rod, which arbitrates the straightness of the neck via an Allen wrench or special truss-rod wrench. A clockwise turn tightens the neck (makes the neck more convex), and a counter-clockwise turn loosens the neck. (Never turn the truss rod more than a quarter turn [12 to 3 on a clock face] in a single adjustment. In fact, don't do this on your own the first time; seek the advice of a professional luthier.)

Frets

Nickel-silver wire (does not contain actual silver, but this is the name of the alloy from which the fret wire is made) that is cut to fit a particular guitar to divide the neck into a series of half steps. For practical, playing purposes, "frets" refer to the spaces between the fret wires. The octave of each open string occurs at the 12th fret, which is often marked with a special fret inlay (usually two dots made from mother-of-pearl).

Body

The resonating chamber of the guitar, often made from several types of wood (too many to discuss here).

Soundhole

The "mouth" of the guitar, often bordered by rings of symmetrical artwork known as a *rosette.*

Bridge

The architecture that connects the body to the strings of the guitar via the saddle, which rests upon the bridge (*ponticello* in Italian).

Saddle

The plastic or bone ridge that rests inside a groove in the bridge and upon which the strings are anchored, usually with a simple single or double knot.

TYPES OF CLASSICAL GUITARS

In broad terms, classical guitars come in two types: *traditional* and *cutaway*. Like most guitars, classical guitars come in different sizes and slightly different shapes, and may use several different woods, even for one part of the guitar.

The photo to the left is a traditional classical guitar made by Kenny Hill, a luthier out of California.

The photo to the right is a Kremona Lulo Reinhardt cutaway guitar made in Bulgaria.

SPECIAL TIMBRAL (TONE) CONSIDERATIONS

Sul Ordinaire: plucking the strings in the ordinary position, just over the lower end of the sound hole. *Sul* means "string"; *ordinaire* means "ordinary" (but you probably figured that out).

Sul Ponticello: plucking the strings by the bridge to generate more treble and a glassy, cold effect. Flamenco players generally play in between *ordinaire* and *ponticello* so the guitar cuts through the sounds of dancers, singers, and percussion.

Sul Tasto: plucking the strings over the neck itself to get a dark, round, warm sound. *Tasto* means "tasty."

VARIOUS CLASSICAL MUSIC TERMINOLOGY

Adagio: a slow tempo; slower than *andante*, but not as slow as *largo*

Allegro: merry, lively tempo

Andante: walking tempo

Animato: animated (relatively quick)

A Tempo: return to original tempo

Crescendo: increase volume

Diminuendo (dim): decrease volume

Espressivo: expressively

Forte *(f)*: loudly

Grazioso: graceful

Largo: very slow tempo with broad and large character

Lento: slow

Luthier: a string-instrument builder and/or repair person

Mezzo Forte *(mf)*: medium volume

Modrato: moderate tempo

Molto: very

Pastorale: work that evokes the countryside

Piano *(p)*: quietly

Pianissimo *(pp)*: very quietly

Poco a poco: little by little

Tres Expressif (French term): with expression

HOW TO READ TAB

As a form of music notation, tab has been around for centuries. However, it has really exploded in popularity among guitar players the past few decades, particularly since the advent of the Internet. The reason for its popularity is the simple fact that it's so easy to learn and use.

A tab staff looks much like a standard treble clef; however, if you look a little closer, you'll notice that it contains *six* lines instead of five. Those six lines represent the six strings of the guitar, with the low-E string positioned at the bottom, and the high-E string at the top. Tab contains no key signature because note-reading is not involved; instead, numbers are placed on the strings to represent the frets of the guitar neck. For example, if you see the number 3 on the low-E (6th) string, you press down on fret 3 of that string. Or if you see a "0" (zero) stacked on the D and G (4th and 3rd) strings, you would pluck those two strings together, open (unfretted).

Sometimes, you'll see tab accompanied by standard notation (like in this book), and other times, you'll see tab-only music. Like standard notation, tab-only music often includes rhythms (stems, flags, beams, rests, etc.). Rhythm symbols in tab are the same as the ones you'll find in standard notation, only the noteheads are replaced by fret numbers.

Regardless of what type of tab is used, a time signature will be present. The *time signature* is a pair of numbers stacked on top of each other at the beginning of a piece of music (immediately after the key signature in standard notation). The top number indicates how many beats comprise each *measure*, or *bar* (the space between the vertical *bar lines*), while the bottom number indicates which note is equivalent to one beat (2 = half note, 4 = quarter note, 8 = eighth note, etc.). Four of the songs in this book are played in 4/4 time, meaning each measure contains four beats (upper number) and quarter notes are equivalent to one beat (bottom number), six songs are played in 3/4 time (each bar contains three beats), one song is in 6/8 time (*six* beats per bar and an eighth note is equivalent to one beat), and one song is in 9/8 time (*nine* beats per bar and an eighth note is equivalent to one beat).

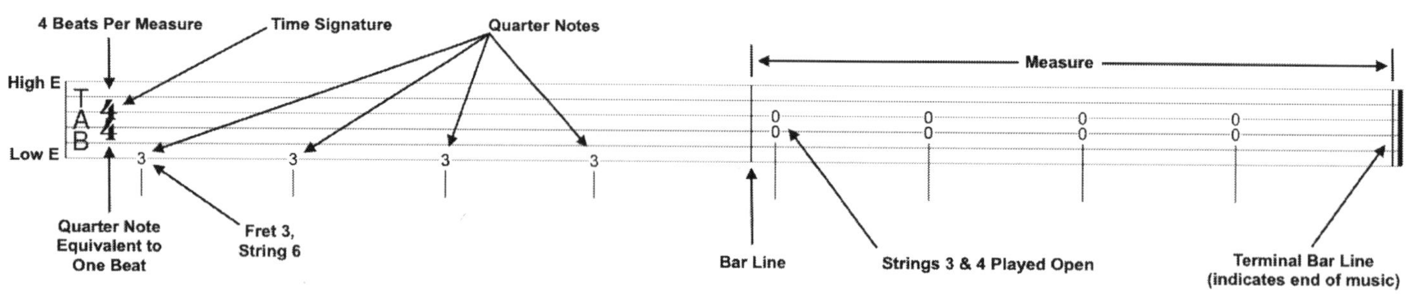

CAPRICE NO. 24

Nicolò Paganini

Although it's presented first in this book (alphabetically), *Caprice No. 24* (*Capriccio No. 24* in Italian), by violin virtuoso Nicolò Paganini, is really the final "boss battle" of this book due to its technical challenges. So, if you feel like your guitar chops aren't ready for this arrangement yet, you can always come back and tackle it at a later date. Alternatively, you can work on it now, just practicing at a *very* slow tempo—even slower than the slow version of the two audio demonstration tracks.

This famous piece—the cornerstone of the *24 Caprices*—established Paganini as the iconic Romantic-era virtuoso violinist and a master of *theme and variations.* The theme (measures 1–8) is not terribly difficult, but that is only part of the beauty of the 24th. The theme is fertile ground for many variations, which Paganini gives us in his virtuosic manifesto. A thematic variation usually retains the same chord progression but alters the melody and rhythms.

I chose some classic—and necessary—picking-hand textures for the variations here (*p–a–m–i* and *p–i–m–i*) that are seen in the works of Giuliani, Sor, and Carcassi, to name a few.

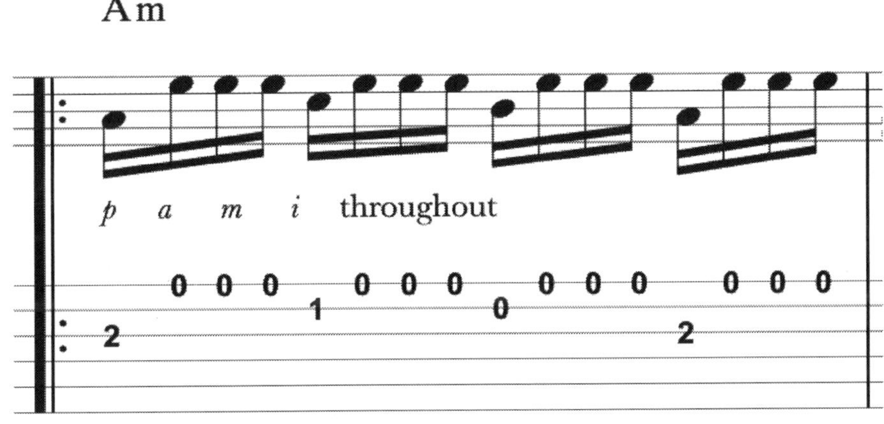

Play this piece slowly and gradually build up speed over weeks—or even months. Don't try to burn this one right away; daily work with a metronome is the way to go.

CAPRICE NO. 24

G7
Am
F7
E7
A5
Am
p a m i throughout
E
Am
E7♭9
A7
p i m i throughout
Dm
G7
C
B°7
C
E7/B
Am
A7
Dm6/F
D♯°7
E7

37
Am/C
Dm
Em
Fmaj7
39
G6
E/G♯
Am
G6
Fmaj7
Em
Dm
C
42
Bm
Asus4
E/G#
Fmaj7#11
E7♭9
rit.
44
Am
E7
Am

CLAIR DE LUNE

Claude Debussy

This is the most famous piece from Claude Debussy's *Bergamasque Suite*, a revised collection of his early piano work. The title simply means "moonlight." Is Debussy referencing Beethoven's *Moonlight Sonata* with this name and by using languid triplets as a rhythmic motif?

Play the piece as legato and relaxed as possible by simply leaving your fret-hand fingers on the notes slightly longer than indicated whenever possible. This arrangement—as with most in this book—provides opportunities to play open strings whenever they are advantageous and musical.

This arrangement has some interesting and tricky rhythmic devices, mostly in the bass (lowest) voice of each chord or phrase. Measures 19–24 use rhythm and volume to spill into the big ending chords. Practice this section slowly and pay special attention to measure 24, as it contains a pretty clear (clair?) *hemiola*, or polyrhythmic, texture (6 over 4 for the first two beats of the measure).

CLAIR DE LUNE

Andante tres Expressif

C Fm C/E

mp

4 Dm F/C G/B Am7 E/G♯

7 C/G F6 C

rit.

A Tempo

10 F6 C/E F6

13 C/E F6 Dsus2

mf

16
2
19
G7
accel.
A♭°7
Dm7/A
22
Bm7♭5
cresc.
F6/C
Dm7
rit.
25
Em
Am7 ♭5
Gsus4
G
f
mf
mp
Harm.
28
Em
Harm.
Cmaj7

CONTESSA PERDONO

Wolfgang Amadeus Mozart

It was difficult to find repertoire from Mozart that can be incorporated into a book with the word "easy" in the title, as Mozart was one of the most freakishly talented musicians to ever walk the Earth. He had not only perfect pitch and a photographic memory, but arguably the most refined musical taste of anyone in the Classical Era (1750–1820), as well. He contrived perfect, complete works in real time and remembered them flawlessly!

I first heard this piece in the film *Amadeus* (1984), from Mozart's opera *The Marriage of Figaro*, and have loved it since. In orchestrating *Contessa* for guitar, I found it necessary to incorporate harmonics, as they offer a drastic, dramatic contrast to the use of heavy open chords (e.g., measures 16–17).

Contessa also offers many opportunities for tonal contrast, from *sul tasto* to *sul ponticello.*
For example, play measures 5–6 *sul tasto*, and then measures 7–8 *sul ponticello* for contrast.

Mozart loved contrast. He also uses constantly shifting dynamics, as seen in the *mezzo piano* (*mp*) to *forte (f)* dynamic shift in measures 10–13.

CONTESSA PERDONO

Adagio

G Dsus4 D

3 D7 Gm(maj7) G G C

6 D7 Em G/B C D7 Em

9 Am G D G G/B C

mp mp mf mp mf mp mf

Harm.

12
D7
Em
G
C
D7
Em
f
15
Am
G
D
G
C
mf
Harm.
f
18
Am
D/F♯
G
Cmaj7
mp
rit.
mf
21
G
D7
1.
G
2.
G
mp

FÜR ELISE

Ludwig van Beethoven

This is probably the most frequently (and incompletely) played "lick" in all the vastness of classical music. Beethoven knew how to embed a motif in the listener's memory, so much so that his melodies are played everywhere today.

The key to playing this arrangement is to form the basic chord shapes right before you play each phrase. This may be the simplest piece in this collection, but it must be played very intentionally, not mechanically.

Also, in measures 16–18, the quasi-cadenza of the opening motif incorporates a 12th-fret E harmonic, which gives the guitarist a little time to return to the lower D♯. Be sure, however, to get the right number of revolutions on the motif, as it's easy to get lost in this phrase.

FÜR ELISE

Freely
rit.
Harm.
A Tempo
Am
E
Am
E
1.
Am
2.
Am
rit.

JESU, JOY OF MAN'S DESIRING

Johann Sebastian Bach

Johann Sebastian Bach's famous and beautiful Christian anthem *Jesu, Joy of Man's Desiring* is often heard in church ceremonies, weddings, and other ritual functions. Originally in 9/8 time, I decided to arrange *Jesu* in 3/4 meter to make the chordal sections easier to read and feel.

Play this piece very slowly until you can easily feel the 3/4 pulse, then try a faster tempo. Don't rush it, though, as this piece seems like it wants to speed up, as do many tunes in triple meters.

The most difficult passage, measures 28–30 (shown below), requires a sudden position shift and a barre with the ring (3rd) finger in measure 29. That said, if you take your time with the shift, practicing it for about 15 minutes, it shouldn't be too difficult.

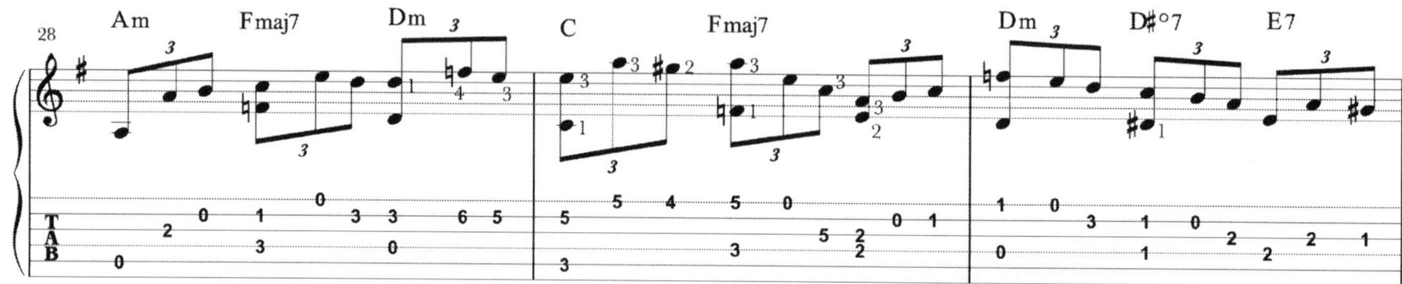

I've played this piece on several wedding gigs over the years and always looked forward to performing it. It was a pleasure to record it here. I hope you enjoy this classic!

JESU, JOY OF MAN'S DESIRING

Andante

16
C6 D6 D G C/E G/B Em
19
Am G/B C6 D7 G Em C
22
G/B Em Em/D C6 C♯m7♭5 D G A7
25
D E7 Am Dm6 Dm7 E7
28
Am Fmaj7 Dm C Fmaj7 Dm D♯°7 E7

31
Am G/B C D/F♯ C G/B
34
C C7 F Dm7 G/B C G/B
37
G G/F♯ C/E G/B Em Am G/B
40
D7/F♯ D7/A G G/F♯ D7/F♯
43
G/B Em D7/C D6 G
rit.
T
A
B

JUPITER
Gustav Holst

This fantastic and epic piece by Gustav Holst is easier than it looks. The key of E is a friendly key to guitarists, the chords are mostly familiar (until the dense structures of the outro), and the tempo is relatively slow. That said, the movement between chords can be a little difficult without proper arrangement, counterpoint, and certain voicings, but I use all of them here to "set up the next shot"—not unlike a game of billiards—so you shouldn't have too much trouble.

For example, note the fingerings and staggered rhythm in measures 14–15, which were simply block chords in the original. This method, however, provides ease of play and rhythm for solo guitar performance.

Measures 10–12 and 26–28 are perhaps the most difficult sections in the piece. I will offer you two ways to play these sections. The first method, shown below, offers less legato, but also less of a stretch.

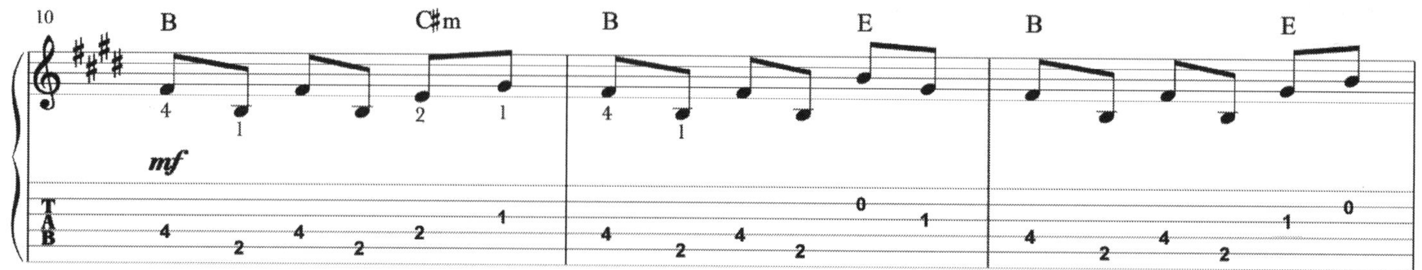

The second method requires a long stretch and a strong pinky, which every player, regardless of genre, needs to develop to be a serious guitarist, but inexperienced players may want to forego this technique if it's too difficult.

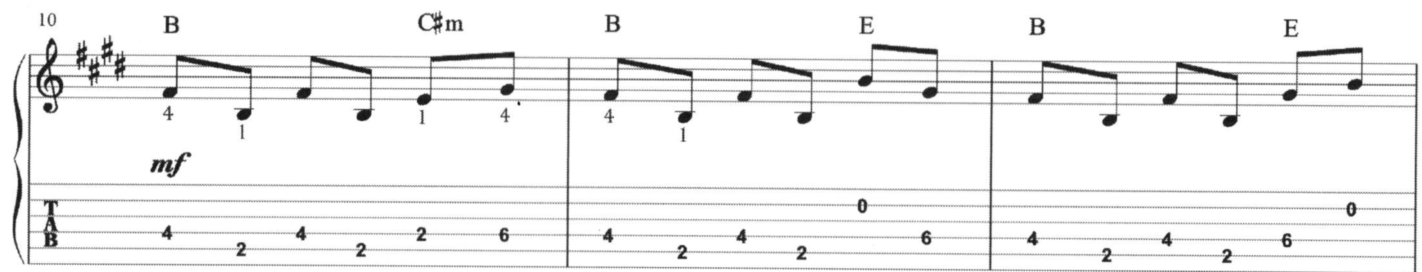

JUPITER

Expressively

A B E

mp

4 A C♯m E A B

7 E/G♯ Amaj7 F♯m E/G♯

Andante Maestoso

10 B C♯m B E B E

mf

13 Amaj7 F♯m7 C♯m G♯m/B A E/G♯ F♯m7 E

16
F♯m/A
C♯m/E
B/D♯
C♯m7
G♯m/B
A
B
19
E/G♯
F♯m
B
C♯m
G♯m/B
22
A
B
E/G♯
Amaj7
F♯m
25
E
B
C♯m
B
E/G♯
28
B
E
Amaj7
f
F♯m
C♯m
G♯m/B
A
31
E/G♯
E/F♯
E
F♯m7
C♯m/E
B
C♯m7
G♯m/B

A
B
E/G#
F#m
B/D#
ff
C#m
E
A
B
E/G#
E
mf
Amaj7
B
Fmaj7/E
G6/E
A/E
Badd11/E
rit.
mf
Emaj7
A6sus2
f
Gently tap strings by bridge
E+
E
Harm.
pp

LULLABY

Johannes Brahms

Johannes Brahms' *Lullaby* is one of the most famous melodies in the world. It's hard to find a person who doesn't know and love this beautiful tune. It evokes the feeling of being tucked in at the end of a beautiful day. Who doesn't need that feeling?

After recording it a few times, I realized how much lighter (and a bit faster) I could—and should—be playing it to evoke a dreamlike state. The real trick to perfecting this arrangement lies in flowing between fretted notes, harmonics, and open strings. Many guitarists compartmentalize these seemingly disparate methods of tone production, making the instrument much more difficult—and less expressive. Harmonics and open strings not only make the guitar more expressive, but also free your fretting hand, allowing time for wide leaps and position shifts.

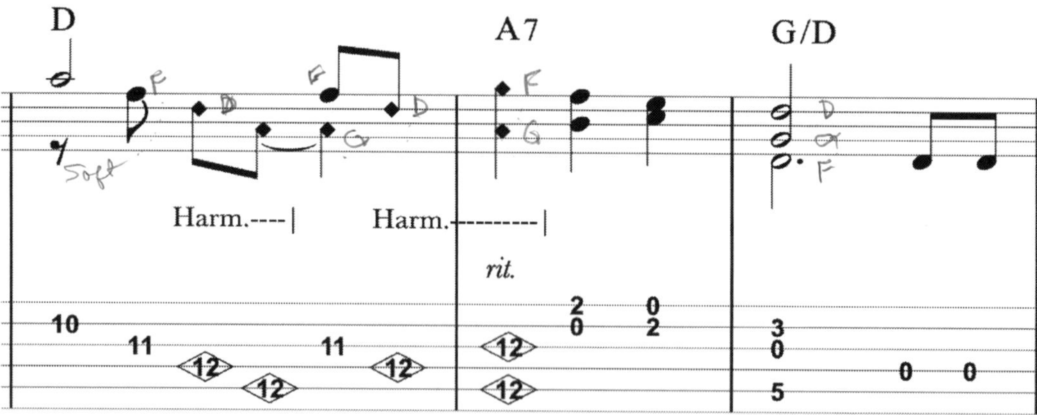

LULLABY

Drop D Tuning

* Detune 6th string from E to D

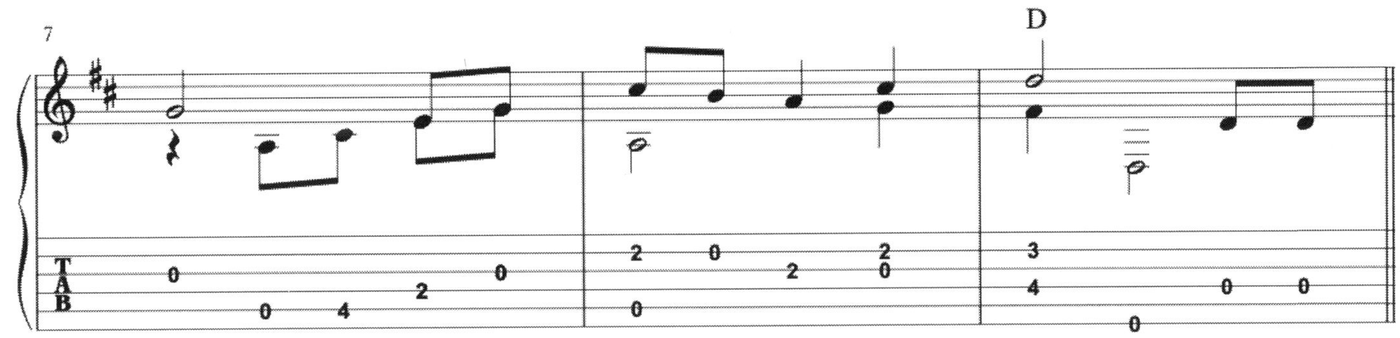

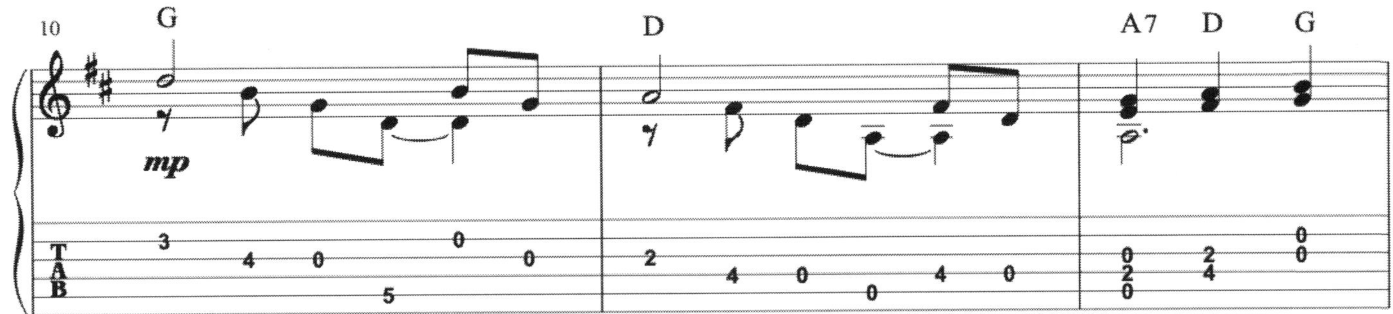

13
D
G
D
16
A7
p
D
18
D
Harm.
Harm.
21
A7
24
D
G
Harm.
mp
Harm.
T
A
B

27
D
A7
D
G
D
Harm.
Harm.--|
Harm.
Harm.------|
30
G
D
A7
G/D
mp
Harm.----|
Harm.----|
Harm.---------|
rit.
34
1.
2.
D

MAZURKA IN A MINOR

Frédéric Chopin

Mazurka in A Minor, named after a Polish dance, is like a little universe unto itself, as there are several regions of varying character and tonality throughout the piece. Personally, my favorite sections are the little cadenzas—usually single-note melodic, improvisatory-sounding passages—that occur throughout.

I've included an extra set of fingerings/tab for measures 14–15 of the second "cadenza" (shown below) to illustrate how much timbral variety can be found on the classical guitar, just by changing the fingerings. This technique is frequently employed by the amazing, eclectic guitarist Bill Frisell.

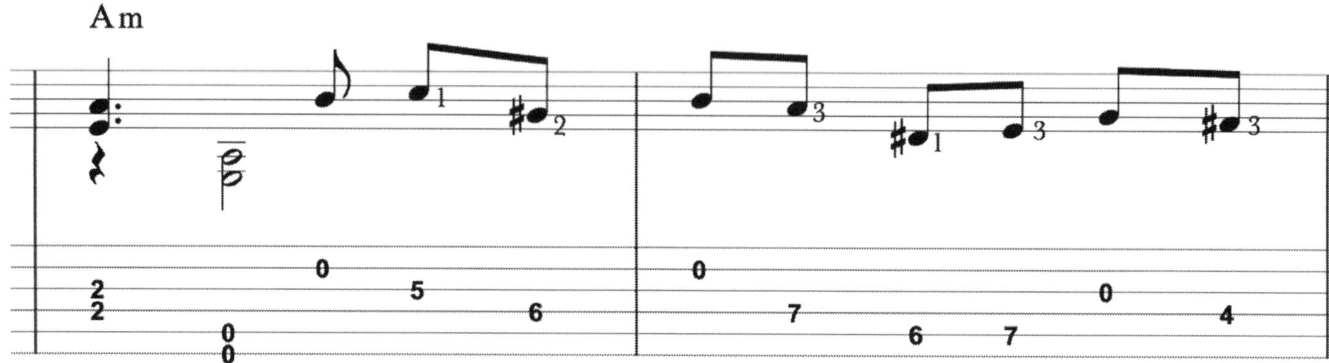

The most difficult part of this *Mazurka* occurs in measures 38–39 (shown below). To make it easier, without loss of musical effect, I simply reduced the low G♯ in bar 39 from a dotted half note to a half note.

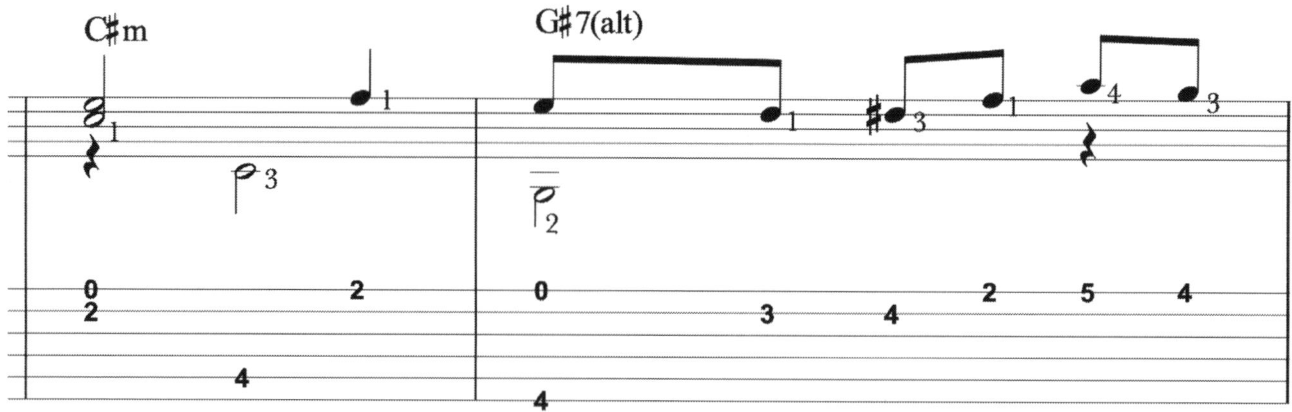

The G♯7(alt) chord is full of *tensions,* a penchant of Chopin and many of the late Romantic-era harmonists. An "alt" symbol in a chord indicates several alterations: ♭5th, ♯5th, ♭9th, and/or ♯9th. In G♯, D is the ♭5th and E (or D double-sharp) is the ♯5th. Note, also, that D♯ is the (regular) 5th, so all three 5ths are present in the melody. Finally, A is the ♭9th, which is also present. So, instead of a chord symbol like G♯7♭5♯5♭9, we simply go with G♯7(alt).

MAZURKA IN A MINOR

Moderato Animato

Am E7

4 Am F/E♭ Am

7 E7 A5

10 Am E7 Am

13 F/E♭ Am

16
E7
Am
B7/E
pp
mp
19
Am
Dm6
E7
Dm
Am
22
G(add9)
Cmaj7
Fadd9
25
Bm7♭5
B7/E
Am
Dm6
E7
cresc.
28
Dm
Am
mf
dim.
31
Sul Tasto
E7
Fine
A5
p

Sul Ordinaire
A
E 13♯11
E
A
C♯m
G♯7(alt)
mp
E/G♯
C♯m
A
E 13♯11
Bm7♭5
E 13
A
F♯7(no3)
D
Bm
cresc.
A/E
rit.
mf
E 7
D.S. al Fine
A 5

MINUET IN G MAJOR

Johann Sebastian Bach

This little gem from the mind of J.S. Bach is one of the world's most well-known melodies. You might not remember where you heard it, but you probably know it.

"Minuet" comes from the French word *menuet*, which means "delicate." In the 1600s, a minuet was a slow, stately dance in two parts, but this piece has gained speed throughout the years. It is often said that a minuet should be around a minute long, so the tempo on this one has a wide range of possibilities.

Don't worry about playing it up to speed right away; just practice very slowly and strive for clean execution. If you do this, you'll soon discover that this piece will pick up speed nicely. To paraphrase Bach: All you have to do is play the right notes at the right time.

The second page is a little more difficult, as you have to get used to playing higher on the neck with open G and D strings for bass notes (even though the open G string is rarely thought of as a bass note). Practice looping measures 17–20 (shown below) for 20 minutes, and you'll have it.

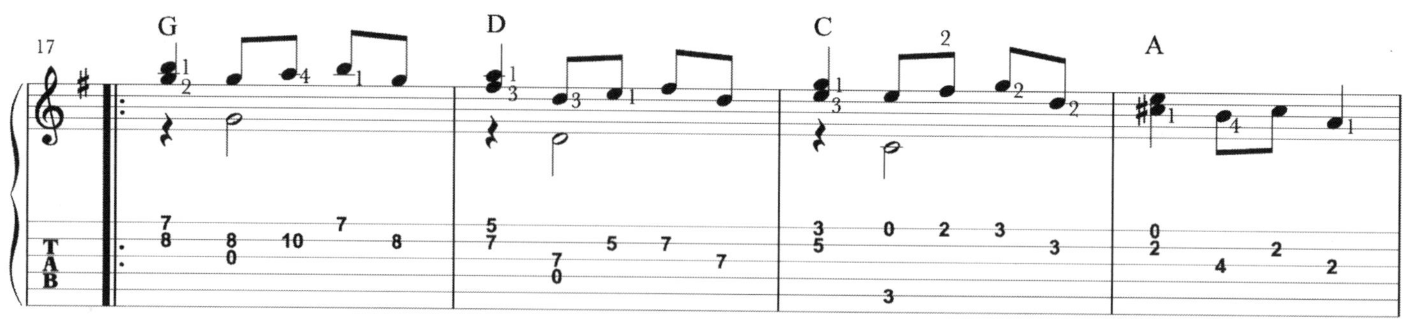

MINUET IN G MAJOR

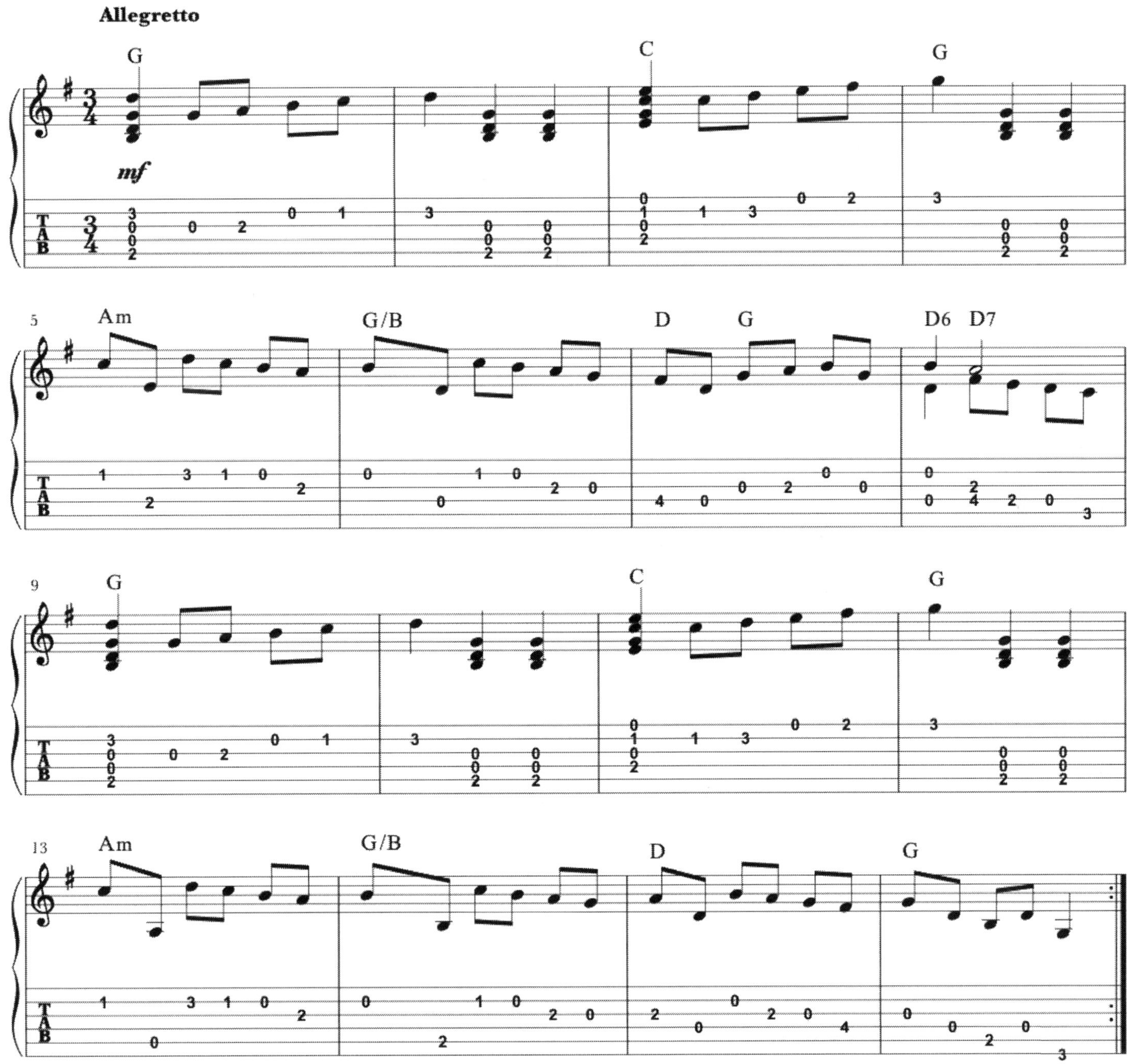

Allegretto

17
G D C A
21
G D/F♯ A/C♯ D A7 D
25
G/B C G D
29
C G D G D7 G
rit.

MORNING MOOD

Edvard Grieg

Morning Mood, or *Morgenstemning i ørkenen* in Norwegian, translates to "morning in the desert," which is not the usual imagery we may visualize, as this piece from the Peer Gynt Suite has been popularized by Warner Bros. cartoons, commercials, and other uses. Here, Peer Gynt is stranded in a Moroccan desert, but surrounded by great, primordial beauty.

The most difficult section of this piece may very well be the *double stops*, or *dyads*, in measures 31–33, but don't worry—there's a strategy to playing these successfully.

The trick is letting the last note stick, as though that finger is stuck to the note from the previous dyad. Don't try to hold down a single chord shape for an entire measure; instead, go slow and let your hand pivot from the remaining note, like the F on the third eighth note of measure 32. In other words, keep your 2nd finger on the F, but let your hand, wrist, and even your elbow pivot on that finger.

Observe the fingerings in the example below, as these will lead you easily through this section.

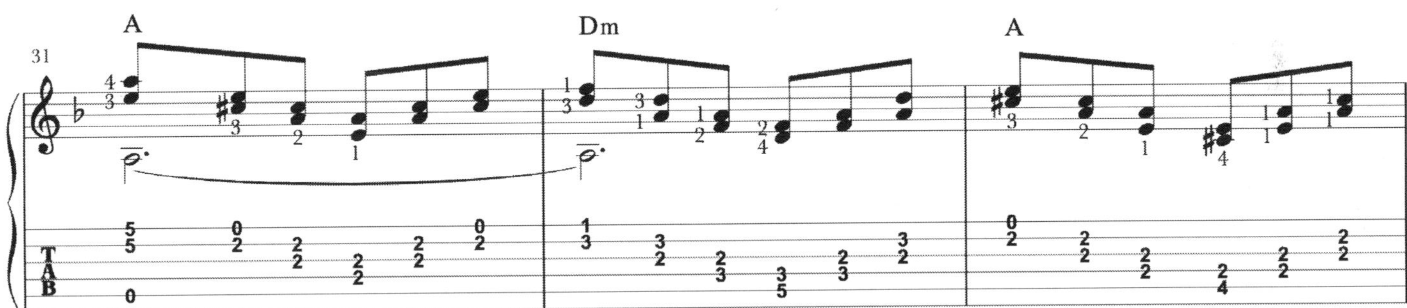

This technique of playing double stops is very common in classical guitar literature. Have fun with the technique and experiment with it via all the chords you already know.

MORNING MOOD

Andante Pastorale

F — Dm

p

4 F

7 Dm — A

mp

10 Gm7 — C

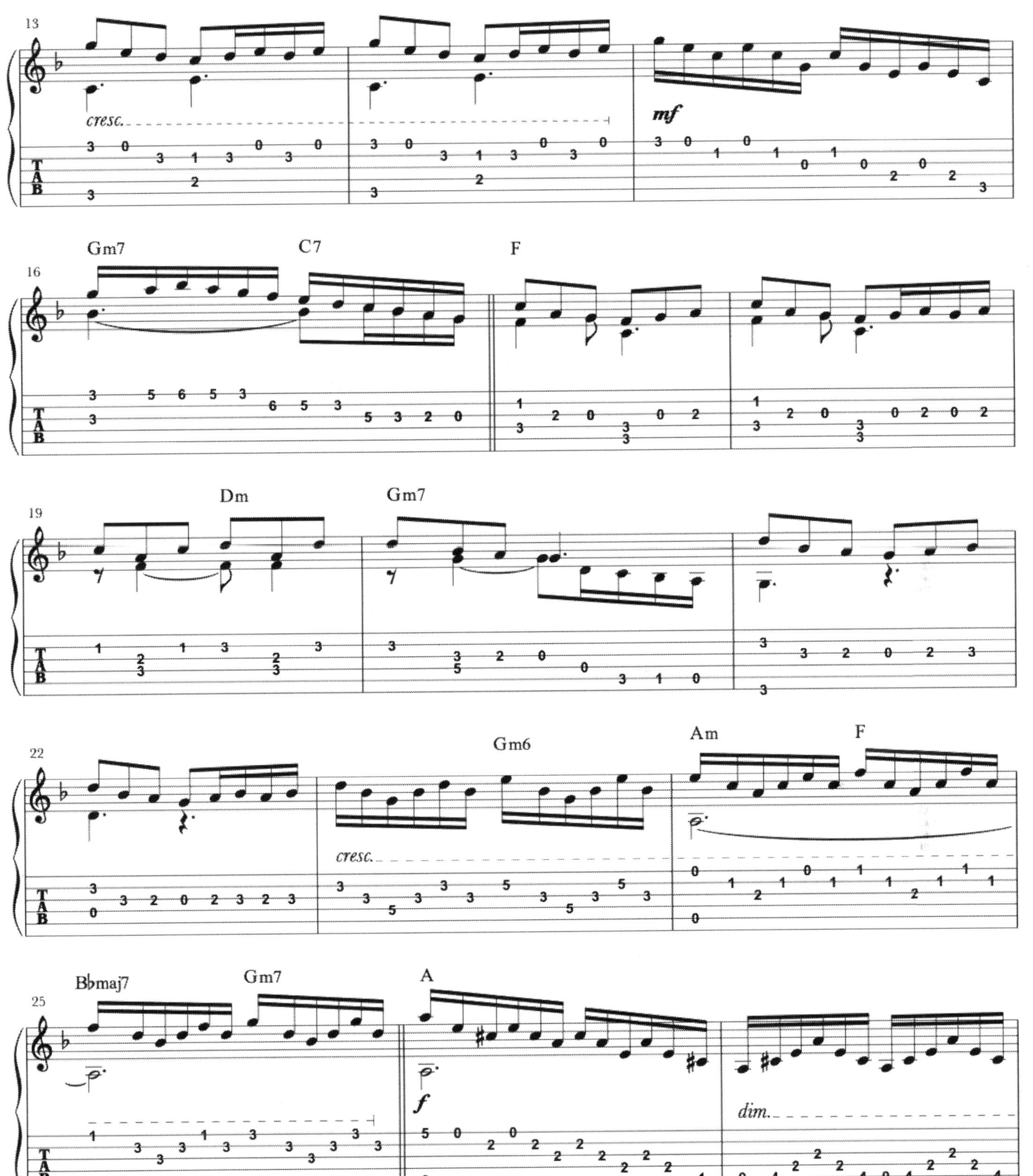
13
cresc.
mf
16
Gm7
C7
F
19
Dm
Gm7
22
Gm6
cresc.
Am
F
25
B♭maj7
Gm7
A
f
dim.

Gm/B♭
A/C♯
Gm/B♭
mf
A
Dm
A
C7
Adagio
F
mp
rit.
Dm/F
A
C7
F
rit.

ODE TO JOY

Ludwig van Beethoven

Here is a different take on Beethoven's famous melody. The intro is slow and somewhat heavy due to the drop-D drone and low arrangement of the melody. Roll the intro chords using your thumb, index, and middle fingers: *p–i–m* (the wavy upwards pointing arrow indicates this type of strum in the notation). I wasn't going to arrange the song like this, but it came out this way and I really like it; it reminds me of a fantastic sunrise. The intro also reminds me of something Chris Cornell might have done.

On the audio, I played measures 9–12 *sul ponticello* to give them a sort of an AM-radio quality to make the entrance of the *presto* section bigger by contrast.

The *presto* section requires a very commonly employed guitar technique: parallel 6ths. Parallel 6ths can be heard in many genres of music from antiquity to the present. Steve Cropper, from Stax Records' house band, Booker T & the MGs, used this technique with Otis Redding, Aretha Franklin, and many others. The interval of a 6th is simply an inverted 3rd, and since the interval of a 3rd controls whether a chord or scale is major or minor, 3rds are arguably the most important set of all the intervals.

Pluck the 6ths in measure 39 (and elsewhere in this piece) with the index and middle fingers in an almost locked-hand position so as to move freely between string groups (high E and G, and B and D).

Study this excerpt from the last five measures, as it contains every technique you will need to play the *presto* section:

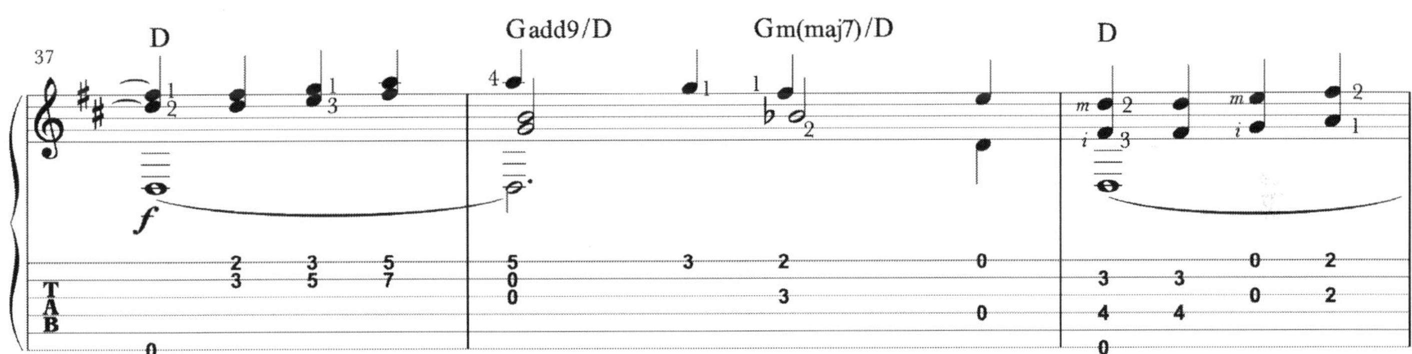

ODE TO JOY

Drop D Tuning

Freely

D A D

mp

* Detune 6th string from E to D.

4 D/A A D Gadd9 Gm(maj7)/B♭

7 D A/C♯ D A D/A

10 A D/A A F♯/A♯ Bm E A D

13
D
Gadd9/B
Gm(maj7)/B♭
D
Presto
16
A/C♯
D
D
A
19
D
A
D
22
Gadd9/D
Gm(maj7)/B♭
D
A7
D
25
A
D/A
A
D/A
A
F♯/A♯

28
Bm E A D
Gadd9/D
Gm(maj7)/B♭
31
D
A7 D
A D/A
mf
34
A D/A
A F♯/A♯
Bm E A D
37
D
f
Gadd9/D
Gm(maj7)/D
D
40
Asus4/D
rit.
A/D
D

PRELUDE IN C MINOR

Frédéric Chopin

Often called the "Chord Prelude," Opus 28, No. 20, or *Prelude in C Minor*, was originally penned in mostly quarter notes, but I decided to notate it in a half-note texture at first, as it seemed to let the score breathe a bit.

The tricky thing about performing the first half of this piece is avoiding string noise, which I managed to do on most of the recording, save for the very last four measures! I felt that the soul of the piece was present on this take, so I left it as is. Perhaps this could be called the "String Noise Prelude." So, where possible, avoid sliding by picking up your fret-hand fingers and "bouncing" to the next chord.

The second half is markedly different from Chopin's original texture, as I felt that the guitar, lacking the sonorous power of the piano, needed more movement to compensate. To ensure flow, I added more linear movement in measures 20 and 24, as well as in the final bar.

The most unusual fingering I ended up using is illustrated below:

The second time through the second page could use a slightly faster tempo and perhaps a slightly different tone (closer to *sul ponticello*, as heard on the recording).

PRELUDE IN C MINOR

17
Cm
A♭
p i m i
mp crescendo poco a poco
18
G/B
Gm/B♭
Am7
A♭7♭5
20
G
Cm
Fm
22
G7
Cm
A♭
D♭
rit.
24
Cm
G7♭9
Cm
G/B
rit.
26
Cm/G
G7♭9
Cm

ABOUT THE AUTHOR

Steve Peplin is an adjunct professor of jazz guitar at Lawrence University in Appleton, Wisconsin, and a full-time instructor at Milwaukee Area Technical College, where he teaches composition, guitar, improvisation, orchestration, and more. He earned an associate's degree in Music Occupations from MATC in 1993, under master jazz guitarist Jack Grassel, and a bachelor's degree in Traditional Composition from Berklee College of Music in 1996.

In addition to teaching, Steve is a member of several bands, including Strangelander, Dinosaur Rocket, Invocation Trio, the Lawrence University Faculty Jazz Ensemble, and others. Steve has also performed with several notable musicians, including Doc Severinsen, Dr. Art Davis (John Coltrane's early bassist), the Milwaukee Symphony Orchestra, the Fox Valley Symphony Orchestra, the Lawrence University Symphony Orchestra, Melvin Rhyne (Wes Montgomery's organist), Dan Trudell, De La Buena, Matchstick, Deirdre Fellner, Dan Schneck, Aaron Gardner, Amanda Huff, Russ Johnson, Jessie Montijo, Carlos Adames, Jamie Breiwick's Choir Fight, and many others.

Made in the USA
Middletown, DE
03 February 2024

49063172R00033